To

Mrs. Emma Moore

From

Evang. Marva C. Norwood
God Bless you & your
entire family

04-03-10

Quiet Reflections: A Mother's Journal
© 2009 Lake House Gifts
A Division of Ellie Claire Gift & Paper Corp.
www.ellieclaire.com

Compiled by Joanie Garborg
Designed by Jeff & Lisa Franke

ISBN 978-1-935416-40-1
Printed in China

Quiet Reflections

A MOTHER'S JOURNAL

LAKE HOUSE

GIFTS

A WORK OF POETRY

*Y*ou wrote no lofty poems
That critics counted art,
But with a nobler vision
You lived them in your heart.

You carved no shapeless marble
To some high soul design,
But with a finer sculpture
You shaped this soul of mine.

You built no great cathedrals
That centuries applaud;
But with a grace exquisite
Your life cathedraled God.

Thomas Fessenden

*N*o song or poem will bear my mother's name.
Yet so many of the stories that I write,
that we all write, are my mother's stories.

Alice Walker

The godly walk with integrity; blessed are their children after them.

PROVERBS 20:7 NLT

A WORK OF POETRY

ETERNALLY PRESENT

*A*s parents feel for their children,
God feels for those who fear him.
He knows us inside and out,
keeps in mind that we're made of mud.
Men and women don't live very long;
like wildflowers they spring up and blossom,
but a storm snuffs them out just as quickly,
leaving nothing to show they were here.
God's love, though, is ever and always,
eternally present to all who fear him,
making everything right for them and their children
as they follow his Covenant ways
and remember to do whatever he said.

Psalm 103:13-18 MSG

*God may be invisible, but He's in touch. You may not be able
to see Him, but He is in control. And that includes all of life—
past, present, future.*

CHARLES R. SWINDOLL

ETERNALLY PRESENT

THE CIRCLE OF LOVE

*B*ecause you love me, I can choose
To look through your dear eyes and see
Beyond the beauty of the Now
Far onward to Eternity.

Because you love me, I can wait
With perfect patience well possessed;
Because you love me, all my life
Is circled with unquestioned rest.

Paul Laurence Dunbar

A mother's love is like a circle, it has no beginning and no ending.
It keeps going around and around ever expanding, touching everyone who
comes in contact with it. Engulfing them like the morning's mist, warming them
like the noontime sun, and covering them like a blanket of evening stars.

Art Urban

*Only the living can praise you…. Each generation can
make known your faithfulness to the next.*

ISAIAH 38:19 NLT

THE CIRCLE OF LOVE

LOVE ONE ANOTHER

*W*atch what God does, and then you do it, like children who learn proper behavior from their parents. Mostly what God does is love you. Keep company with him and learn a life of love. Observe how Christ loved us. His love was not cautious but extravagant. He didn't love in order to get something from us but to give everything of himself to us. Love like that.

Ephesians 5:1–2 MSG

I pray that your love for each other will overflow more and more, and that you will keep on growing in your knowledge and understanding.

Philippians 1:9 NLT

Open your hearts to the love God instills....
God loves you tenderly. What He gives you is not to
be kept under lock and key, but to be shared.

MOTHER TERESA

LOVE ONE ANOTHER

CHILD OF GOD

When we call on God, He bends down His ear to listen,
as a mother bends down to listen to her little child.

Elizabeth Charles

He only is the Maker
of all things near and far;
He paints the wayside flower,
He lights the evening star;
the wind and waves obey Him,
by Him the birds are fed;
much more to us, His children,
He gives our daily bread.

Matthias Claudius

Remember you are very special to God as His
precious child. He has promised to complete the good work
He has begun in you. As you continue to grow in Him,
He will make you a blessing to others.

Since God so loved us, we also ought to love one another.

1 JOHN 4:11 NIV

CHILD OF GOD

TO ALL GENERATIONS

*K*now therefore that the Lord your God is God; he is the
faithful God, keeping his covenant of love to a thousand
generations of those who love him and keep his commands.

Deuteronomy 7:9 NIV

*F*or the Lord is good; his mercy is everlasting;
and his truth endureth to all generations....
Thy kingdom is an everlasting kingdom,
and thy dominion endureth throughout all generations.

Psalm 100:5; 145:13 KJV

I will sing of the mercies of the Lord for ever: with my mouth
will I make known thy faithfulness to all generations.

Psalm 89:1 KJV

*In following our everlasting God,
we touch the things that last forever.*

To All Generations

BEAUTIFUL INFLUENCE

She has a more influential and powerful role than any political, military, religious or educational figure. Her words are never fully forgotten. If you were blessed with a good mother, you will enjoy the advantages for the rest of your days. If your mother neglected you and her responsibilities, unfortunately the impact is almost certainly still felt today. For good or for ill, a mother's impact is permanent. A child's mother is arguably the most influential figure in his or her life, giving credence to the old adage: the hand that rocks the cradle rules the world.

Blessed is the influence of one true, loving human soul on another.

George Eliot (Mary Ann Evans)

There is no influence so powerful as that of the mother.

Sarah Joseph Hale

Place these words on your hearts.
Get them deep inside you.... Teach them to your children.
DEUTERONOMY 11:18-19 MSG

BEAUTIFUL INFLUENCE

DELIGHT IN THE LORD

*D*elight yourself in the Lord and he will give you
the desires of your heart. Commit your way to
the Lord; trust in him and he will do this:
He will make your righteousness shine like the dawn,
the justice of your cause like the noonday sun.

Psalm 37:4-6 NIV

*S*end forth your light and your truth, let them guide me;
let them bring me to your holy mountain,
to the place where you dwell. Then will I go to the
altar of God, to God, my joy and my delight.

Psalm 43:3-4 NIV

*Our fulfillment comes in knowing God's glory,
loving Him for it, and delighting in it.*

DELIGHT IN THE LORD

GRACE REVEALED

*L*ook deep within yourself and recognize what
brings life and grace into your heart.
It is this that can be shared with those around you.
You are loved by God. This is an inspiration to love.

Christopher de Vinck

*A*ll God's glory and beauty come from within, and there
He delights to dwell. His visits there are frequent, His conversation sweet,
His comforts refreshing, His peace passing all understanding.

Thomas à Kempis

*T*he Lord's chief desire is to reveal Himself to you and, in order
for Him to do that, He gives you abundant grace. The Lord gives you
the experience of enjoying His presence. He touches you, and His touch
is so delightful that, more than ever, you are drawn inwardly to Him.

Madame Jeanne Guyon

*Set your hope fully on the grace to be given
you when Jesus Christ is revealed.*

1 PETER 1:13 NIV

GRACE REVEALED

CONTENTMENT

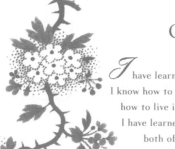

I have learned to be content in whatever circumstances I am.
I know how to get along with humble means, and I also know
how to live in prosperity; in any and every circumstance
I have learned the secret of being filled and going hungry,
both of having abundance and suffering need.
I can do all things through Him who strengthens me.

Philippians 4:11–13 NASB

*B*e content with who you are, and don't put on airs.
God's strong hand is on you; he'll promote you at the right time.
Live carefree before God; he is most careful with you.

1 Peter 5:6–7 MSG

*G*odliness with contentment is great gain. For we brought
nothing into the world, and we can take nothing out of it.
But if we have food and clothing, we will be content with that.

1 Timothy 6:6–8 NIV

Contentment is not the fulfillment of what you want,
but the realization of how much you already have.

Contentment

Time to Cherish

*A*t the end of your life you will never regret not having
passed one more test, not winning one more verdict,
or not closing one more deal. You will regret time not spent
with a spouse, a friend, a child, or a parent.

Barbara Bush

*C*hildren will not remember you for
the material things you provided,
but for the feeling that you cherished them.

Gail Grenier Sweet

*E*very material goal, even if it is met, will pass away.
But the heritage of children is timeless.
Our children are our messages to the future.

Billy Graham

May the Lord richly bless both you and your children.
May you be blessed by the Lord, who made heaven and earth.

P S A L M   1 1 5 : 1 4 - 1 5   N L T

TIME TO CHERISH

TENDER LOVE

*F*or all God's words are right, and everything he does
is worthy of our trust. He loves whatever is just and good;
the earth is filled with his tender love.

Psalm 33:4–5 TLB

*F*or, lo, the winter is past, the rain is over and gone;
the flowers appear on the earth;
the time of the singing of birds is come.

Song of Solomon 2:11–12 KJV

*H*e has remembered his love and his faithfulness...
all the ends of the earth have seen the salvation of our God.

Psalm 98:3 NIV

*Love is the sweet, tender, melting nature of God flowing into
the creature, making the creature most like unto himself.*

ISAAC PENNINGTON

TENDER LOVE

JOY IS...

*J*oy is the touch of God's finger. The object of our
longing is not the touch but the Toucher.
This is true of all good things—they are all God's touch.
Whatever we desire, we are really desiring God.

Peter Kreeft

*J*oy is really a road sign pointing us to God.
Once we have found God...we no longer need to
trouble ourselves so much about the quest for joy.

C. S. Lewis

*J*oy is the echo of God's life within us.

Now the God of hope fill you with all joy and peace in believing.

ROMANS 15:13 KJV

JOY IS...

MY HELP

I will lift up mine eyes unto the hills, from whence
cometh my help. My help cometh from the Lord,
which made heaven and earth. He will not suffer thy foot
to be moved: he that keepeth thee will not slumber.
Behold, he that keepeth Israel shall neither slumber
nor sleep. The Lord is thy keeper: the Lord is thy
shade upon thy right hand. The sun shall not smite
thee by day, nor the moon by night. The Lord shall preserve thee
from all evil: he shall preserve thy soul. The Lord shall preserve thy
going out and thy coming in from this time forth, and even for evermore.

Psalm 121:1-8 KJV

We have a Father in heaven who is almighty, who loves His children
as He loves His only-begotten Son, and whose very joy and delight
it is to...help them at all times and under all circumstances.

GEORGE MUELLER

MY HELP

FOOTPRINTS

I cannot name myself as one
Who never goes astray,
Who never stumbles on the road,
Or leaves the hallowed way.
But when I know that baby feet
Will follow where I've trod,
I walk with care that they too may walk
That road that leads to God.

Margaret Fishback Powers

*T*he walks and talks we have with our two-year-olds in red boots
have a great deal to do with the values they will cherish as adults.

Edith F. Hunter

Even children are known by the way they act,
whether their conduct is pure and right.

PROVERBS 20:11 NLT

FOOTPRINTS

LOVE ONE ANOTHER

*C*lothe yourselves with compassion, kindness,
humility, gentleness and patience. Bear with each other
and forgive whatever grievances you may have against
one another. Forgive as the Lord forgave you.
And over all these virtues put on love,
which binds them all together in perfect unity.

Colossians 3:12-14 NIV

A new command I give you: Love one another.
As I have loved you, so you must love one another.

John 13:34 NIV

*M*ay God, who gives this patience and encouragement,
help you live in complete harmony with each other.

Romans 15:5 NLT

*In God's wisdom, He frequently chooses to meet our needs by showing
His love toward us through the hands and hearts of others.*

JACK HAYFORD

LOVE ONE ANOTHER

COUNTLESS BEAUTIES

*M*ay God give you eyes to see beauty only the heart
can understand. From the world we see, hear, and touch,
we behold inspired visions that reveal God's glory.
In the sun's light, we catch warm rays of grace and
glimpse His eternal design. In the birds' song,
we hear His voice and it reawakens our
desire for Him. At the wind's touch,
we feel His Spirit and sense our eternal existence.

*A*ll the world is an utterance of the Almighty. Its countless beauties,
its exquisite adaptations, all speak to you of Him.

Phillips Brooks

Worship the Lord in the beauty of holiness.

PSALM 96:9 NIV

COUNTLESS BEAUTIES

EACH NEW CHANCE

*G*od made my life complete when
I placed all the pieces before him....
God rewrote the text of my life
when I opened the book of my heart to his eyes.

Psalm 18:20, 24 MSG

*N*ow the God of peace...make you perfect in every
good work to do his will, working in you that which
is wellpleasing in his sight, through Jesus Christ;
to whom be glory for ever and ever. Amen.

Hebrews 13:20-21 KJV

*God puts each fresh morning, each new chance of life,
into our hands as a gift.*

EACH NEW CHANCE

OLD-FASHIONED LOVE

*H*er heart is like her garden,
Old-fashioned, quaint and sweet.
With here a wealth of blossoms,
And there a still retreat.

Alice E. Allen

*R*ejecting things because they are old-fashioned would
rule out the sun and the moon, and a mother's love.

*I*f there be one thing pure...that can endure,
when all else passes away...it is a mother's love.

Marchioness de Spadara

For this is the message that ye heard from the beginning,
that we should love one another.

1 JOHN 3:11 KJV

OLD-FASHIONED LOVE

OF GREAT VALUE

*A*re not five sparrows sold for two pennies?
Yet not one of them is forgotten by God. Indeed, the very
hairs of your head are all numbered. Don't be afraid;
you are worth more than many sparrows.

Luke 12:6–7 NIV

*F*or God bought you with a high price.
So you must honor God with your body.

1 Corinthians 6:20 NLT

*F*or you know that it was not with perishable things
such as silver or gold that you were redeemed...but with the
precious blood of Christ, a lamb without blemish or defect.

1 Peter 1:18–19 NIV

*You are in the Beloved...therefore infinitely dear
to the Father, unspeakably precious to Him.*

NORMAN F. DOWTY

OF GREAT VALUE

....

....

....

....

....

....

....

....

....

....

....

....

....

....

....

....

....

....

FAITH ADVENTURE

*T*here will always be the unknown. There will always be
the unprovable. But faith confronts those frontiers with
a thrilling leap. Then life becomes vibrant with adventure!

Robert Schuller

*F*aith means you want God and want
to want nothing else.... In faith there is movement
and development. Each day something is new.

Brennan Manning

*F*aith sees the invisible, believes the incredible,
and receives the impossible.

*F*aith is not a sense, not sight, not reason,
but a taking God at His Word.

Evans

For with God all things are possible.

MARK 10:27 KJV

FAITH ADVENTURE

GOD'S THOUGHTS

*Y*our thoughts—how rare, how beautiful! God,
I'll never comprehend them! I couldn't even
begin to count them—any more than I could count
the sand of the sea. Oh, let me rise in the morning
and live always with you!

Psalm 139:17–18 MSG

*T*he counsel of the Lord standeth for ever,
the thoughts of his heart to all generations.

Psalm 33:11 KJV

*H*ow great are your works, O Lord,
how profound your thoughts!

Psalm 92:5 NIV

*W*hy do you say..."My way is hidden from the Lord;
my cause is disregarded by my God"? Do you not know?
Have you not heard? The Lord is the everlasting God,
the Creator of the ends of the earth. He will not grow tired
or weary, and his understanding no one can fathom.

Isaiah 40:27–28 NIV

*Just when we least expect it, He intrudes into our neat
and tidy notions about who He is and how He works.*

JONI EARECKSON TADA

GOD'S THOUGHTS

CAPACITY FOR CARING

*G*od sends children for another purpose than merely to
keep up the race—to enlarge our hearts, to make us
unselfish, and full of kindly sympathies and affections;
to give our souls higher aims, to call out all our faculties
to extended enterprise and exertion; to bring round
our fireside bright faces and happy smiles, and loving,
tender hearts. My soul blesses the Great Father every day,
that He has gladdened the earth with little children.

Mary Howitt

A cheerful giver does not count the cost of what she gives. Her heart
is set on pleasing and cheering the one to whom the gift is given.

Julian of Norwich

*T*he capacity for caring illuminates any relationship.
The more people you care about, and the more intensely you care,
the more alive you are.

*Finally, all of you should be of one mind, full of
sympathy toward each other, loving one another
with tender hearts and humble minds.*

1 PETER 3:8 NLT

CAPACITY FOR CARING

THE NEXT GENERATION

O my people, hear my teaching;
listen to the words of my mouth.
I will open my mouth in parables,
I will utter hidden things, things from of old—
what we have heard and known,
what our fathers have told us.
We will not hide them from their children;
we will tell the next generation
the praiseworthy deeds of the Lord,
his power, and the wonders he has done...
which he commanded our forefathers
to teach their children,
so the next generation would know them,
even the children yet to be born,
and they in turn would tell their children.
Then they would put their trust in God
and would not forget his deeds
but would keep his commands.

Psalm 78:1–7 NIV

Teach your children why you believe what you believe....
Don't be afraid to teach them to think for themselves.
God's Word can withstand the test.

PAUL MEIER

THE NEXT GENERATION

His Imprint

*T*he God of the universe – the One who created everything and holds it all in His hand – created each of us in His image, to bear His likeness, His imprint. It is only when Christ dwells within our hearts, radiating the pure light of His love through our humanity that we discover who we are and what we were intended to be.

*I*n the very beginning it was God who formed us by His Word. He made us in His own image. God was spirit and He gave us a spirit so that He could come into us and mingle His own life with our life.

Madame Jeanne Guyon

*M*ade in His image, we can have real meaning, and we can have real knowledge through what He has communicated to us.

Francis Schaeffer

For in Him all the fullness of Deity dwells in bodily form,
and in Him you have been made complete.

Colossians 2:9 NASB

HIS IMPRINT

WATER OF LIFE

*F*or I will pour water on the thirsty land, and streams
on the dry ground; I will pour out my Spirit on
your offspring, and my blessing on your descendants.
They will spring up like grass in a meadow,
like poplar trees by flowing streams.

Isaiah 44:3–4 NIV

*T*he earth shall be filled with the knowledge of the
glory of the Lord, as the waters cover the sea.

Habakkuk 2:14 KJV

*I*s anyone thirsty? Come!
All who will, come and drink,
Drink freely of the Water of Life!

Revelation 22:17 MSG

*Jesus...has been waiting all along for us to bring our needy
selves to Him and receive from Him that eternal water.*

DORIS GAILEY

WATER OF LIFE

PURE AFFECTION

*W*hat is Mother's love?
A noble, pure, and tender flame
Enkindled from above.

James Montgomery

*S*omehow she made possible for me my truest affections,
as an act of great literature would bestow upon its devoted reader.
And I have known that moment with her we would all like to know,
the moment of saying, "Yes. This is what it is."
An act of knowing that certifies love.

Richard Ford

I would give more for the private esteem and love of one
than for the public praise of ten thousand.

W. E. Alger

*O*ne of life's greatest treasures is the love that binds
mother and child together in friendship.

Love each other with genuine affection,
and take delight in honoring each other.

ROMANS 12:10 NLT

PURE AFFECTION

GOD'S WORD

*W*ith my whole heart have I sought thee:
O let me not wander from thy commandments.
Thy word have I hid in mine heart, that I might not
sin against thee.... I will not forget thy word.

Psalm 119:10–11, 16 KJV

*A*ll Scripture is God-breathed and is useful for teaching,
rebuking, correcting and training in righteousness.

2 Timothy 3:16 NIV

*F*or the word of God is living and active and sharper than any
two-edged sword, and piercing as far as the division of soul and spirit,
of both joints and marrow, and able to judge the thoughts and intentions
of the heart. And there is no creature hidden from His sight, but all things
are open and laid bare to the eyes·of Him with whom we have to do.

Hebrews 4:12–13 NASB

*When we give the Word of God space to live in our heart,
the Spirit of God will use it to take root,
penetrating the earthiest recesses of our lives.*

KEN GIRE

GOD'S WORD

A LIFE TRANSFORMED

*T*o pray is to change. This is a great grace.
How good of God to provide a path whereby our lives
can be taken over by love and joy and peace
and patience and kindness and goodness and
faithfulness and gentleness and self-control.

Richard J. Foster

*F*or God is, indeed, a wonderful Father who longs to pour out
His mercy upon us, and whose majesty is so great that
He can transform us from deep within.

Teresa of Avila

A life transformed by the power of God
is always a marvel and a miracle.

Geraldine Nicholas

Create in me a clean heart, O God;
and renew a right spirit within me.

PSALM 51:10 KJV

A LIFE TRANSFORMED

SHEPHERD AND GUARDIAN

*H*e shall feed his flock like a shepherd:
he shall gather the lambs with his arm,
and carry them in his bosom,
and shall gently lead those that are with young.

Isaiah 40:11 KJV

*A*ll we like sheep have gone astray;
we have turned every one to his own way;
and the Lord hath laid on him the iniquity of us all.

Isaiah 53:6 KJV

*Y*ou were continually straying like sheep, but now you have
returned to the Shepherd and Guardian of your souls.

1 Peter 2:25 NASB

*Genuine love sees faces, not a mass: the Good Shepherd
calls His own sheep by name.*

GEORGE A. BUTTRICK

SHEPHERD AND GUARDIAN

A FOUNDATION FOR LIFE

We all belong to another world, to another time,
to another place of long ago. I believe it is
important to share your history with those you
love so that they will be able to tell their
children about the foundation of their lives.

Christopher de Vinck

If our children have the background of a godly, happy home
and this unshakable faith that the Bible is indeed the Word of God,
they will have a foundation that the forces of hell cannot shake.

Ruth Bell Graham

For whatever life holds for you and your family in the coming days,
weave the unfailing fabric of God's Word through your heart and mind.
It will hold strong, even if the rest of life unravels.

Gigi Graham Tchividjian

It takes wisdom to build a house,
and understanding to set it on a firm foundation.

PROVERBS 24:3 MSG

A FOUNDATION FOR LIFE

EXPECTANT REVERENCE

God is within all things, but not included;
outside all things, but not excluded,
above all things, but not beyond their reach.

Pope St. Gregory I

There is a unique kind of transparence about
things and events. The world is seen through,
and no veil can conceal God completely. So those who
are pious are ever alert to see behind the appearance
of things a trace of the divine, and thus their attitude
toward life is one of expectant reverence.

Abraham Joshua Heschel

Because God created the Natural—invented it out of
His love and artistry—it demands our reverence.

C. S. Lewis

*But for you who revere my name, the sun of righteousness
will rise with healing in its wings.*

MALACHI 4:2 NIV

EXPECTANT REVERENCE

EVER PRESENT

*W*hen I walk by the wayside, He is along with me....
Amid all my forgetfulness of Him, He never forgets me.

Thomas Chalmers

*T*here's not a tint that paints the rose
Or decks the lily fair,
Or marks the humblest flower that grows,
But God has placed it there....
There's not a place on earth's vast round,
In ocean's deep or air,
Where love and beauty are not found,
For God is everywhere.

*A*t every moment, God is calling your name and waiting to be found.
To each cry of "Oh Lord," God answers, "I am here."

God is our refuge and strength, an ever-present help in trouble.
Therefore we will not fear.

PSALM 46:1-2 NIV

EVER PRESENT

SEEK FIRST

$\mathcal{L}$ook at the birds of the air, that they do not sow,
nor reap nor gather into barns, and yet your heavenly
Father feeds them. Are you not worth much more than they?
And who of you by being worried can add a single hour
to his life? And why are you worried about clothing?
Observe how the lilies of the field grow; they do not
toil nor do they spin, yet I say to you that not even Solomon
in all his glory clothed himself like one of these. But if God
so clothes the grass of the field, which is alive today and
tomorrow is thrown into the furnace, will He not much more
clothe you? You of little faith! Do not worry then, saying,
"What will we eat?" or "What will we drink?" or "What will we
wear for clothing?" For...your heavenly Father knows
that you need all these things. But seek first His kingdom
and His righteousness, and all these things will be added to you.

Matthew 6:26-33 NASB

Trust the past to the mercy of God, the present to His love,
and the future to His Providence.

AUGUSTINE

SEEK FIRST

A MOTHER'S HEART

*T*here is in all this world no fount of deep, strong,
deathless love, save that within a mother's heart.

Felicia Hemans

*D*issect a mother's heart and see
The properties it doth contain—
What pearls of love, what gems of hope—
A mother's heart beats not in vain.

Caleb Dunn

*T*he world is full of riches, but none of them can compare
with the treasures that lie within a mother's heart.

Patricia H. Rushford

A mother's heart is always with her children.

As a mother comforts her child, so will I comfort you.

ISAIAH 66:13 NIV

A Mother's Heart

A RIVER OF DELIGHTS

*Y*our love, O Lord,
reaches to the heavens,
your faithfulness to the skies.
Your righteousness
is like the mighty mountains,
your justice like the great deep....
How priceless is your unfailing love!
Both high and low among men
find refuge in the shadow of your wings.
They feast on the abundance
of your house;
you give them drink
from your river of delights.
For with you is the fountain of life;
in your light we see light.

Psalm 36:5-9 NIV

*God's love is like a river springing up in the Divine Substance
and flowing endlessly through His creation, filling all things
with life and goodness and strength.*

THOMAS MERTON

A RIVER OF DELIGHTS

MIRACLE OF GRACE

*F*ace your deficiencies and acknowledge them....
Let them teach you patience, sweetness, insight.
When we do the best we can, we never know what miracle
is wrought in our life, or in the life of another.

Helen Keller

*W*hen the soul has laid down its faults at the feet of God,
it feels as though it had wings.

Eugenie de Guerin

*W*here there is faith, there is love.
Where there is love, there is peace.
Where there is peace, there is God.
Where there is God, there is no need.

And God is able to make all grace abound to you,
so that in all things at all times, having all that you need,
you will abound in every good work.

2 CORINTHIANS 9:8 NIV

MIRACLE OF GRACE

LIVE IN HARMONY

*T*he wisdom that comes from heaven is first of all pure.
It is also peace loving, gentle at all times, and willing
to yield to others. It is full of mercy and good deeds.
It shows no partiality and is always sincere.

James 3:17 NLT

*F*inally, all of you, live in harmony with one another;
be sympathetic, love..., be compassionate and humble.
Do not repay evil with evil or insult with insult,
but with blessing, because to this you were called
so that you may inherit a blessing.

1 Peter 3:8-9 NIV

*To love other people means to see them
as God intended them to be.*

Live in Harmony

THE REFUGE OF HOME

*B*y home, we mean a place in which the mind can settle;
where it is too much at ease to be inclined to rove;
a refuge to which we flee in the expectation of finding
those calm pleasures, those soothing kindnesses,
which are the sweetness of life.

James Bean

A loving relationship is home for one's soul—
a place to be ourselves and explore our deepest
inner yearnings, hopes, fears, and joys, without fear
of condemnation, rejection, or being abandoned.

Leo Buscaglia

*A*n important part of the domestic policy of every mother
should be to make her children feel that home is the
happiest place in the world. This delicious home-feeling
is one of the choicest gifts a parent can bestow.

He blesses the home of the righteous.

PROVERBS 3:33 NIV

THE REFUGE OF HOME

THE LORD'S PRAYER

*O*ur Father
which art in heaven,
Hallowed be thy name.
Thy kingdom come:
Thy will be done in earth,
as it is in heaven.
Give us this day our daily bread.
And forgive us our debts,
as we forgive our debtors.
And lead us not into temptation,
but deliver us from evil:
For thine is the kingdom,
and the power,
and the glory,
for ever.
Amen.

Matthew 6:9–13 KJV

They who seek the throne of grace find that throne in every place;
If we live a life of prayer, God is present everywhere.

OLIVER HOLDEN

THE LORD'S PRAYER

DREAMS FULFILLED

*L*ift up your eyes. Your heavenly Father
waits to bless you — in inconceivable ways to make
your life what you never dreamed it could be.

Anne Ortlund

*G*od created us with an overwhelming desire to soar....
He designed us to be tremendously productive and
"to mount up with wings like eagles," realistically
dreaming of what He can do with our potential.

Carol Kent

*T*he human heart, has hidden treasures,
In secret kept, in silence sealed; —
The thoughts, the hopes, the dreams, the pleasures,
Whose charms were broken if revealed.

Charlotte Brontë

*I'll lead you to buried treasures, secret caches of valuables —
Confirmations that it is, in fact, I, God... who calls you by your name.*

ISAIAH 45:3 MSG

DREAMS FULFILLED

THE GARDEN OF MY LIFE

*A*t that same time, a fine vineyard will appear.
There's something to sing about! I, God, tend it.
I keep it well-watered. I keep careful watch over it
so that no one can damage it.... Even if it gives me
thistles and thornbushes, I'll just pull them out
and burn them up. Let that vine cling to me
for safety, let it find a good and whole life with me,
let it hold on for a good and whole life.

Isaiah 27:2–5 MSG

*A*bide in Me, and I in you. As the branch cannot
bear fruit of itself unless it abides in the vine,
so neither can you unless you abide in Me. I am the vine,
you are the branches; he who abides in Me and I in him,
he bears much fruit, for apart from Me you can do nothing.

John 15:4–5 NASB

*It is God's knowledge of me, His careful husbanding
of the ground of my being, His constant presence in the
garden of my little life that guarantees my joy.*

W. PHILLIP KELLER

THE GARDEN OF MY LIFE

A WOMAN SET APART

*T*here will be singing in your heart,
There will be a rapture in your eyes;
You will be a woman set apart,
You will be so wonderful and wise.

Robert W. Service

*M*other—in this consists the glory
and the most precious ornament of woman.

Martin Luther

*T*he sweetest sounds to mortals given
are heard in Mother, Home, and Heaven.

W. G. Brown

Her children arise up, and call her blessed.

P R O V E R B S 3 1 : 2 8 K J V

A WOMAN SET APART

THE WORD OF GOD

*F*or as the rain cometh down, and the snow from heaven,
and returneth not thither, but watereth the earth,
and maketh it bring forth and bud, that it may give seed
to the sower, and bread to the eater: So shall my word
be that goeth forth out of my mouth: it shall not
return unto me void, but it shall accomplish that which
I please, and it shall prosper in the thing whereto I sent it.

Isaiah 55:10–11 KJV

*N*ot one word has failed of all His good promise.

1 Kings 8:56 NASB

God is the God of promise. He keeps His word,
even when that seems impossible.
COLIN URQUHART

THE WORD OF GOD

IN HIS IMAGE

*G*od's designs regarding you, and His methods of
bringing about these designs, are infinitely wise.

Madame Jeanne Guyon

*S*tand outside this evening.
Look at the stars. Know that you are special
and loved by the One who created them.

*A*ll that we have and are is one of the unique and
never-to-be repeated ways God has chosen to express
himself in space and time. Each of us, made in
His image and likeness, is yet another promise He has made
to the universe that He will continue to love it and care for it.

Brennan Manning

*So God created people in his own image; God patterned them
after himself; male and female he created them.*

GENESIS 1:27 NLT

In His Image

THE LOVE OF GOD

*W*ho shall separate us from the love of Christ?
Shall trouble or hardship or persecution or famine or
nakedness or danger or sword?... No, in all these things
we are more than conquerors through him who loved us.
For I am convinced that neither death nor life,
neither angels nor demons, neither the present nor
the future, nor any powers, neither height nor depth,
nor anything else in all creation, will be able to separate us
from the love of God that is in Christ Jesus our Lord.

Romans 8:35–39 NIV

*Nothing can separate you from His love, absolutely nothing.... God is
enough for time, and God is enough for eternity. God is enough!*

HANNAH WHITALL SMITH

THE LOVE OF GOD

STANDING BY EACH OTHER

A mother is the truest friend we have when trials,
    heavy and sudden, fall upon us;
    when adversity takes the place of prosperity.

Washington Irving

T hen come the wild weather, come sleet or snow,
    We will stand by each other, however it blow.

Simon Dach

I know of no realm of life that can provide more companionship
    in a lonely world or greater feelings of security
    and purpose in chaotic times than the close ties of a family.

Charles R. Swindoll

I t is the family that gives us a deep private sense of belonging.
    Here we first begin to have our self defined for us.

Howard Thurman

*Be humble and gentle. Be patient with each other, making allowance
for each other's faults because of your love.*

EPHESIANS 4:2 NLT

STANDING BY EACH OTHER

FRUIT IN SEASON

*W*hat happens when we live God's way? He brings gifts
into our lives, much the same way that fruit appears in
an orchard—things like affection for others, exuberance
about life, serenity. We develop a willingness
to stick with things, a sense of compassion
in the heart, and a conviction that a basic
holiness permeates things and people.

Galatians 5:22–23 MSG

*O*h, the joys of those who do not follow the advice
of the wicked, or stand around with sinners, or join in with scoffers.
But they delight in doing everything the Lord wants; day and
night they think about his law. They are like trees planted along
the riverbank, bearing fruit each season without fail.
Their leaves never wither, and in all they do, they prosper.

Psalm 1:1–3 NLT

Love is a fruit in season at all times,
and within the reach of every hand.

MOTHER TERESA

Fruit in Season

GOD DRAWS NEAR

*W*hen you are lonely I wish you love;
When you are down I wish you joy;
When you are troubled I wish you peace;
When things are complicated I wish you simple beauty;
When things are chaotic I wish you inner silence;
When things seem empty I wish you hope,
And the sweet sense of God's presence every passing day.

*G*od still draws near to us in the ordinary, commonplace,
everyday experiences and places.... He comes in surprising ways.

Henry Gariepy

*I have set the Lord always before me: because he is
at my right hand, I shall not be moved.*

PSALM 16:8 KJV

GOD DRAWS NEAR

PROTECTION

*T*he Lord is my light and my salvation—whom shall I fear?
The Lord is the stronghold of my life—of whom shall
I be afraid?... One thing I ask of the Lord,
this is what I seek: that I may dwell in the house of
the Lord all the days of my life, to gaze upon
the beauty of the Lord and to seek him in his temple.
For in the day of trouble he will keep me safe in his
dwelling; he will hide me in the shelter of his tabernacle
and set me high upon a rock.... Hear my voice when I call,
O Lord; be merciful to me and answer me. My heart says
of you, "Seek his face!" Your face, Lord, I will seek.

Psalm 27:1, 4–5, 7–8 NIV

Leave behind your fear and dwell on the lovingkindness of God,
that you may move forward with your eyes fixed on Him.

PROTECTION

GUIDING LIGHT

*M*y mother was the source from which
I derived the guiding principles of my life.

John Wesley

A mother's guidance will sharpen your character,
draw your soul into the light, and challenge
your heart to love in a greater way.

A MOTHER'S PRAYER

*O*h God, You have given me a vacant soul, an untaught conscience,
a life of clay. Put Your big hands around mine and guide my hands
so that every time I make a mark on this life, it will be Your mark.

Gloria Gaither

I would lead you and bring you to my mother's house—
she who has taught me.

SONG OF SONGS 8:2 NIV

GUIDING LIGHT

FAITH IS...

*N*ow faith is being sure of what we hope for and certain of what we do not see.... By faith we understand that the universe was formed at God's command, so that what is seen was not made out of what was visible.... And without faith it is impossible to please God, because anyone who comes to him must believe that he exists and that he rewards those who earnestly seek him.

Hebrews 11:1, 3, 6 NIV

Faith, as the Bible defines it, is present-tense action. Faith means being sure of what we hope for...now. It means knowing something is real, this moment, all around you, even when you don't see it. Great faith isn't the ability to believe long and far into the misty future. It's simply taking God at His word and taking the next step.

JONI EARECKSON TADA

FAITH IS...

HIS PRESENCE

*A*nd I have felt
A presence that disturbs me with the joy
Of elevated thoughts; a sense sublime
Of something far more deeply interfused,
Whose dwelling is the light of setting suns.

William Wordsworth

*K*now by the light of faith that God is present,
and be content with directing all your actions toward Him.

Brother Lawrence

*G*od wants us to be present where we are.
He invites us to see and to hear what is around us and,
through it all, to discern the footprints of the Holy.

Richard J. Foster

*If I rise on the wings of the dawn, if I settle on the far side of the sea,
even there your hand will guide me, your right hand will hold me fast.*

PSALM 139:9-10 NIV

HIS PRESENCE

....

....

....

....

....

....

....

....

....

....

....

....

....

....

....

....

....

GOD'S WAYS

O the depth of the riches both of the wisdom
and knowledge of God! how unsearchable
are his judgments, and his ways past finding out!
For who hath known the mind of the Lord?
or who hath been his counsellor?

Romans 11:33-34 KJV

*F*or my thoughts are not your thoughts,
neither are your ways my ways, saith the Lord.
For as the heavens are higher than the earth,
so are my ways higher than your ways,
and my thoughts than your thoughts.

Isaiah 55:8-9 KJV

*In both simple and eloquent ways, our infinite God personally
reveals glimpses of himself in the finite.*

GOD'S WAYS

THE RHYTHM OF LOVE

*F*athers and mothers, husbands, wives, or children,
or the company of earthly friends, are but shadows,
but God is the substance. These are but
scattered beams, but God is the sun.
These are but streams. But God is the ocean.

Jonathan Edwards

*G*od loves me as God loves all people, without qualification....
To be in the image of God means that all of us are
made for the purpose of knowing and loving God
and one another and of being loved in turn.

Roberta Bondi

*F*rom the heart of God comes the strongest rhythm—
the rhythm of love. Without His love reverberating in us,
whatever we do will come across like a noisy gong or a
clanging cymbal. And so the work of the human heart, it seems
to me, is to listen for that music and pick up on its rhythms.

Ken Gire

*How great is the love the Father has lavished on us, that we should
be called children of God! And that is what we are!*

1 JOHN 3:1 NIV

THE RHYTHM OF LOVE

CHILDREN'S CHILDREN

*I*n ages past you laid the foundation of the earth,
and the heavens are the work of your hands.
Even they will perish, but you remain forever;
they will wear out like old clothing. You will change
them like a garment, and they will fade away.
But you are always the same; your years never end.
The children of your people will live in security.
Their children's children will thrive in your presence.

Psalm 102:25–28 NLT

*O*h, that their hearts would be inclined to fear me
and keep all my commands always, so that it
might go well with them and their children forever!

Deuteronomy 5:29 NLT

*The resource from which He gives is boundless, measureless,
unlimited, unending, abundant, almighty, and eternal.*

JACK HAYFORD

CHILDREN'S CHILDREN

HIS BEAUTIFUL WORLD

*T*he God who holds the whole world in His hands
wraps himself in the splendor of the
sun's light and walks among the clouds.

*F*orbid that I should walk through Thy beautiful
world with unseeing eyes:
Forbid that the lure of the market-place should ever entirely steal
my heart away from the love of the open acres and the green trees:
Forbid that under the low roof of workshop or office or study
I should ever forget Thy great overarching sky.

John Baillie

*O*ur Creator would never have made such lovely days, and given us the deep hearts to
enjoy them, above and beyond all thought, unless we were meant to be immortal.

Nathaniel Hawthorne

The whole earth is full of his glory.

ISAIAH 6:3 KJV

His Beautiful·World

As Good as His Word

*N*ot one word of all the good words which
the Lord your God spoke concerning
you has failed; all have been fulfilled for you,
not one of them has failed.

Joshua 23:14 NASB

*T*he fulfillment of God's promise depends entirely on
trusting God and his way, and then simply embracing
him and what he does. God's promise arrives as pure gift.

Romans 4:16 MSG

*Y*our promises have been thoroughly tested;
that is why I love them so much.

Psalm 119:140 NLT

We may...depend upon God's promises, for...
He will be as good as His word.

MATTHEW HENRY

As Good as His Word

MYSTERY AND WONDER

*T*here is nothing more thrilling in this world,
I think, than having a child that is yours,
and yet is mysteriously a stranger.

Agatha Christie

A baby is...Unwritten history! Unfathomed mystery!

Josiah Gilbert Holland

*I*f children are to retain their innate sense of wonder, they need
at least one adult who can share it with them, rediscovering
the joy, excitement, and mystery of the world we live in.

A child is...an island of curiosity surrounded by a sea of question marks.

*Y*ou hold within your words the power to help your children
feel important and have more meaningful life experiences.

Doug Fields

*Let the little children come to me, and do not hinder them,
for the kingdom of heaven belongs to such as these.*

MATTHEW 19:14 NIV

MYSTERY AND WONDER

BOUNDLESS STRENGTH

I ask the God of our Master, Jesus Christ,
the God of glory—to make you intelligent and
discerning in knowing him personally, your eyes focused
and clear, so that you can see exactly what it is he is
calling you to do, grasp the immensity of this
glorious way of life he has for Christians, oh,
the utter extravagance of his work in us who trust him—
endless energy, boundless strength!

Ephesians 1:17–19 MSG

*T*he Lord is great, and greatly to be praised....
The Lord made the heavens. Honour and majesty are before him:
strength and beauty are in his sanctuary....
Give unto the Lord glory and strength.
Give unto the Lord the glory due unto his name.

Psalm 96:4–8 KJV

*Strength, rest, guidance, grace, help, sympathy, love—
all from God to us! What a list of blessings!*
EVELYN STENBOCK

BOUNDLESS STRENGTH

TOTALLY AWARE

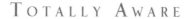

*G*od is every moment totally aware of each one of us.
Totally aware in intense concentration and love....
No one passes through any area of life, happy or tragic,
without the attention of God with him.

Eugenia Price

*B*ecause God is responsible for our welfare, we are told to cast
all our care upon Him, for He cares for us. God says, "I'll take
the burden—don't give it a thought—leave it to Me." God is keenly
aware that we are dependent upon Him for life's necessities.

Billy Graham

*Y*ou are God's created beauty and the focus of His affection and delight.

Janet L. Weaver Smith

Cast thy burden upon the Lord, and he shall sustain thee.

PSALM 55:22 KJV

TOTALLY AWARE

ROADS TO TRAVEL

*I*f you want to live well, make sure you understand
all of this. If you know what's good for you,
you'll learn this inside and out.
God's paths get you where you want to go.
Right-living people walk them easily; wrong-living
people are always tripping and stumbling.

Hosea 14:9 MSG

*E*nter through the narrow gate. For wide is the gate and
broad is the road that leads to destruction,
and many enter through it. But small is the gate and narrow
the road that leads to life, and only a few find it.

Matthew 7:13 NIV

*A*nd how blessed all those in whom you live, whose lives
become roads you travel; they wind through lonesome valleys,
come upon brooks, discover cool springs and pools
brimming with rain! God-traveled, these roads curve
up the mountain, and at the last turn—Zion! God in full view!

Psalm 84:5–7 MSG

*Heaven often seems distant and unknown, but if He who made
the road...is our guide, we need not fear to lose the way.*

HENRY VAN DYKE

ROADS TO TRAVEL

TO MOTHER

*F*or childhood's golden memories
For happy bygone years
The comfort of your presence
In days of joy or tears
For all your love upon life's way—
I thank you from my heart this day.

*W*ho is it that loves me and will love me forever
with an affection which no chance, no misery,
no crime of mine can do away? It is you, my mother.

Thomas Carlyle

*N*o love could be more steadfast,
No heart more kind and true,
No mother in the world could be
More precious and dear than you.

In the house of the righteous is much treasure.

PROVERBS 15:6 KJV

To Mother

GOD'S CARE

*T*he Lord is my shepherd; I shall not want.
He maketh me to lie down in green pastures:
he leadeth me beside the still waters.
He restoreth my soul: he leadeth me in the
paths of righteousness for his name's sake.
Yea, though I walk through the valley of the
shadow of death, I will fear no evil: for thou art
with me; thy rod and thy staff they comfort me.
Thou preparest a table before me in the presence
of mine enemies: thou anointest my head with oil;
my cup runneth over. Surely goodness and
mercy shall follow me all the days of my life:
and I will dwell in the house of the Lord for ever.

Psalm 23:1-6 KJV

*God never abandons anyone on whom He has set His love; nor does
Christ, the good shepherd, ever lose track of His sheep.*

J. I. PACKER

GOD'S CARE

ENFOLDED IN PEACE

I will let God's peace infuse every part of today.
As the chaos swirls and life's demands pull at me on
all sides, I will breathe in God's peace that surpasses all
understanding. He has promised that He would set
within me a peace too deeply planted to be affected
by unexpected or exhausting demands.

*C*alm me, O Lord, as you stilled the storm,
Still me, O Lord, keep me from harm.
Let all the tumult within me cease,
Enfold me, Lord, in your peace.

Celtic Traditional

*G*od cannot give us a happiness and peace apart from himself,
because it is not there. There is no such thing.

C. S. Lewis

*God's peace...is far more wonderful than the human
mind can understand. His peace will keep your
thoughts and your hearts quiet and at rest.*

PHILIPPIANS 4:7 TLB

ENFOLDED IN PEACE

Our Gracious God

*T*he Lord longs to be gracious to you;
he rises to show you compassion.
For the Lord is a God of justice.
Blessed are all who wait for him!

Isaiah 30:18 NIV

*H*e made known his ways to Moses,
his deeds to the people of Israel:
The Lord is compassionate and gracious,
slow to anger, abounding in love.

Psalm 103:7–8 NIV

O Lord, be gracious to us; we long for you.
Be our strength every morning,
our salvation in time of distress.

Isaiah 33:2 NIV

*Lord...give me only Your love and Your grace. With this I am
rich enough, and I have no more to ask.*

Ignatius of Loyola

OUR GRACIOUS GOD

LASTING LEGACIES

*T*here are two lasting legacies we can give our children.
One of these is roots; the other, wings.

*T*he future destiny of the child is always
the work of the mother.

Napoleon Bonaparte

I long to put the experience of fifty years at once into your
young lives, to give you at once the key of that treasure chamber
every gem of which has cost me tears and struggles and prayers,
but you must work for these inward treasures yourself.

Harriet Beecher Stowe

*Y*ou may not be able to leave your children a great inheritance,
but day by day you may be weaving coats for them
which they will wear through all eternity.

T. L. Cuyler

Don't you see that children are God's best gift?
the fruit of the womb his generous legacy?

PSALM 127:3 MSG

LASTING LEGACIES

THE FAITHFULNESS OF GOD

*Y*ou, O God, are both tender and kind, not easily angered,
immense in love, and you never, never quit.

Psalm 86:15 MSG

*I*t is good to give thanks to the Lord and to sing
praises to Your name, O Most High; to declare Your
lovingkindness in the morning and Your faithfulness by night.

Psalm 92:1–2 NASB

*F*or the Lord God is a sun and shield; the Lord gives grace and glory;
no good thing does He withhold from those who walk uprightly.

Psalm 84:10–11 NASB

*T*he Lord is righteous...He will do no injustice. Every morning
He brings His justice to light; He does not fail.

Zephaniah 3:5 NASB

*God takes care of His own…. At just the right moment He
steps in and proves himself as our faithful heavenly Father.*

CHARLES R. SWINDOLL

THE FAITHFULNESS OF GOD

BY LOVE ALONE

*B*y love alone is God enjoyed;
by love alone delighted in,
by love alone approached and admired.
His nature requires love.

Thomas Traherne

*L*ove does not allow lovers
to belong anymore to themselves,
but they belong only to the Beloved.

Dionysius

*T*here is an essential connection between experiencing God,
loving God, and trusting God. You will trust God only as much
as you love Him, and you will love Him to the extent you
have touched Him, rather that He has touched you.

Brennan Manning

*Love the Lord your God with all your heart,
all your soul, and all your strength.*

DEUTERONOMY 6:5 NLT

BY LOVE ALONE

THE PROMISE OF REST

*T*he promise of "arrival" and "rest" is still there
for God's people. God himself is at rest. And at the end
of the journey we'll surely rest with God. So let's keep
at it and eventually arrive at the place of rest.

Hebrews 4:9–11 MSG

*C*ome unto me, all ye that labour and are heavy laden,
and I will give you rest. Take my yoke upon you, and learn of me;
for I am meek and lowly in heart: and ye shall find rest
unto your souls. For my yoke is easy, and my burden is light.

Matthew 11:28–30 KJV

I will refresh the weary and satisfy the faint.

Jeremiah 31:25 NIV

In His arms He carries us all day long.

FANNY J. CROSBY

THE PROMISE OF REST

AN EXPRESSION OF GOD

*T*here is a religion in all deep love,
but the love of a mother is the veil of a softer light
between the heart and the heavenly Father.

Samuel Taylor Coleridge

*T*he way from God to a human heart
is through a human heart.

S. D. Gordon

*W*e have not made ourselves; we are the gift
of the living God to one another.

Reine Duell Bethany

*A*ll that I have and all that I do
is nothing compared to God's love for you.

*T*here is no greater pleasure than bringing to the
uncluttered, supple mind of a child the delight of knowing
God and the many rich things He has given us to enjoy.

Gladys M. Hunt

*If we love each other, God lives in us, and his love has been
brought to full expression through us.*

1 JOHN 4:12 NLT

An Expression of God

SEEN AND UNSEEN

*F*or the truth about God is known to them instinctively. God has put this knowledge in their hearts. From the time the world was created, people have seen the earth and sky and all that God made. They can clearly see his invisible qualities—his eternal power and divine nature. So they have no excuse whatsoever for not knowing God.

Romans 1:19-20 NLT

*A*m I not present everywhere, whether seen or unseen?

Jeremiah 23:24 MSG

*S*o we fix our eyes not on what is seen, but on what is unseen. For what is seen is temporary, but what is unseen is eternal.

2 Corinthians 4:18 NIV

Live with eternity's values in view.

SEEN AND UNSEEN

THE GOODNESS OF GOD

*T*he goodness of God is infinitely more
wonderful than we will ever be able to comprehend.

A. W. Tozer

*A*ll that is good, all that is true,
all that is beautiful, all that is beneficent,
be it great or small, be it perfect or fragmentary,
natural as well as supernatural,
moral as well as material, comes from God.

John Henry Newman

*W*e walk without fear, full of hope and courage and strength
to do His will, waiting for the endless good which He
is always giving as fast as He can get us able to take it in.

George MacDonald

*Open your mouth and taste, open your eyes and see—
how good God is. Blessed are you who run to him. Worship God
if you want the best; worship opens doors to all his goodness.*

PSALM 34:8-9 MSG

THE GOODNESS OF GOD

GOD'S FAVOR

*T*he Spirit of the Sovereign Lord is on me,
because the Lord has anointed me to preach
good news to the poor. He has sent me to bind up the
brokenhearted, to proclaim freedom for the captives
and release from darkness for the prisoners,
to proclaim the year of the Lord's favor and the
day of vengeance of our God, to comfort all who mourn,
and provide for those who grieve in Zion—to bestow on
them a crown of beauty instead of ashes, the oil of gladness
instead of mourning, and a garment of praise instead
of a spirit of despair. They will be called oaks of righteousness,
a planting of the Lord for the display of his splendor.

Isaiah 61:1–3 NIV

God longs to give favor—that is, spiritual strength and health—
to those who seek Him, and Him alone...in order to make His
holy beauty and His great redeeming power known.

TERESA OF AVILA

GOD'S FAVOR

THE POWER OF
MOTHERHOOD

*B*lessings on the hand of women!
Fathers, sons, and daughters cry,
And the sacred song is mingled
With the worship in the sky—
Mingles where no tempest darkens,
Rainbows evermore are hurled;
For the hand that rocks the cradle
Is the hand that rules the world.

William Ross Wallace

*F*or the mother is and must be, whether she knows it or not,
the greatest, strongest, and most lasting teacher her children have.

Hannah Whitall Smith

*N*o language can express the power and beauty
and heroism and majesty of a mother's love.

Edwin Hubbell Chapin

*And let us consider how we may spur one another
on toward love and good deeds.*

HEBREWS 10:24 NIV

The Power of Motherhood

A PERSONAL GUIDE

*B*ut I'll take the hand of those who don't know
the way, who can't see where they're going.
I'll be a personal guide to them, directing them through
unknown country. I'll be right there to show them
what roads to take, make sure they don't fall
into the ditch. These are the things I'll be doing for
them—sticking with them, not leaving them for a minute.

Isaiah 42:16 MSG

*W*hether you turn to the right or to the left,
your ears will hear a voice behind you, saying,
"This is the way; walk in it."

Isaiah 30:21 NIV

*W*e can make our plans,
but the Lord determines our steps.

Proverbs 16:9 NLT

We have ample evidence that the Lord is able to guide.
The promises cover every imaginable situation.
All we need to do is to take the hand He stretches out.

ELISABETH ELLIOT

A PERSONAL GUIDE

A LIFE OF PURPOSE

*R*ecognizing who we are in Christ and aligning
our life with God's purpose for us gives a sense
of destiny.... It gives form and direction to our life.

Jean Fleming

*W*hen we live life centered around what others like,
feel, and say, we lose touch with our own identity.
I am an eternal being, created by God.
I am an individual with purpose. It's not what I get from life,
but who I am, that makes the difference.

Neva Coyle

*G*od has a purpose for your life and no one else can take your place.

The Lord will fulfill his purpose for me;
your love, O Lord, endures forever—
do not abandon the works of your hands.

PSALM 138:8 NIV

A LIFE OF PURPOSE

SHOW YOUR SPLENDOR

*S*atisfy us in the morning with your unfailing love,
that we may sing for joy and be glad all our days.
Make us glad for as many days as you have afflicted us,
for as many years as we have seen trouble.
May your deeds be shown to your servants,
your splendor to their children.
May the favor of the Lord our God rest upon us;
establish the work of our hands for us—
yes, establish the work of our hands.

Psalm 90:14–17 NIV

*Today Jesus is working just as wonderful works as when He
created the heaven and the earth. His wondrous grace, His wonderful
omnipotence, is for His child who trusts Him, even today.*

CHARLES E. HURLBURT AND T. C. HORTON

Show Your Splendor

REAL LOVE

*I*f you would have your children to walk honorably
through the world, you must not attempt to clear
the stones from their path, but teach them to
walk firmly over them—not to insist on leading
them by the hand, but let them learn to go alone.

Anne Brontë

*W*omen can do no greater thing than to create the climate
of love in their homes. Love which spoils and pampers,
weakens and hampers. Real love strengthens and matures
and leaves the loved one free to grow.

Eugenia Price

*T*he mother loves her children most divinely, not when she
surrounds them with comfort and anticipates their wants,
but when she resolutely holds them to the highest standards
and is content with nothing less than their best.

Mabie Hamilton Wright

Love one another deeply, from the heart.

1 PETER 1:22 NIV